Jam Session

Mark McGwire

Terri Dougherty
ABDO Publishing Company

visit us at
www.abdopub.com

Published by ABDO Publishing Company, 4940 Viking Drive, Suite 622, Edina, Minnesota 55435.

Printed in the United States.

Cover and Interior Photo credits: AP/Wide World Photos

Edited by Denis Dougherty

Sources: Associated Press; Chicago Tribune; New York Daily News; Sports Illustrated; Sports Illustrated For Kids; Time Magazine; Washington Post

Library of Congress Cataloging-in-Publication Data

Dougherty, Terri.
    Mark McGwire / Terri Dougherty.
        p. cm. -- (Jam Session)
    Includes index.
    Summary: Presents a biography of the St. Louis Cardinal slugger who broke Roger Maris' single-season home run record in 1998.
    ISBN 1-57765-349-1 (hardcover)
    ISBN 1-57765-347-5 (paperback)
    1. McGwire, Mark, 1963- --Juvenile literature.   2. Baseball players--United States--Biography--Juvenile literature. [1. McGwire, Mark, 1963- . 2. Baseball players.]
    I. Title. II. Series.
    GV865.M396D68   1999
    796.357'092--dc21
    [B]
                                       98-43248
                                         CIP
                                       AC

Contents

New Home Run Hero

It was a historic blast, but not a typical home run by Mark McGwire's standards. The ball zoomed 341 feet straight across Busch Stadium in St. Louis, barely making it over the left field wall. Even Mark wasn't certain it would clear the fence. But when it sailed over, he leaped into the air and pumped his fist. He was so excited he jumped right over first base and had to go back to touch the bag.

Mark was elated as he practically floated around the bases. The St. Louis Cardinals slugger's 62nd home run of the year had broken former New York Yankees star Roger Maris' record of 61. The record had stood for 37 years.

"I was so shocked," Mark said on the magical night of September 8, 1998. "I didn't think the ball had enough to get out."

An emotional crowd cheered Mark's record-setting fourth-inning home run off the Chicago Cubs' Steve Trachsel. After rounding the bases, Mark was mobbed by teammates. He lifted his 10-year-old son, Matthew, a Cardinals batboy, into the air and kissed him.

The Cubs' Sammy Sosa, who was also chasing Maris' record, came in from right field to congratulate Mark. Mark then went into the stands and hugged Maris' children. He later emerged from the dugout and addressed the buzzing crowd. "To all my family, my son, the Cubs, Sammy Sosa," he said. "It's unbelievable."

Incredibly, Mark still had 18 games to go after he broke Maris' record. "I've been talking about this since January," Mark said after the game. "All of a sudden it's here—I can say I did it.

"The last week and a half my stomach has been turning, my heart has been beating a million miles a minute. To do it that fast—I don't know—I just give thanks to the man upstairs and all of them, Roger Maris, Babe Ruth, everybody who is watching up there. What a feat."

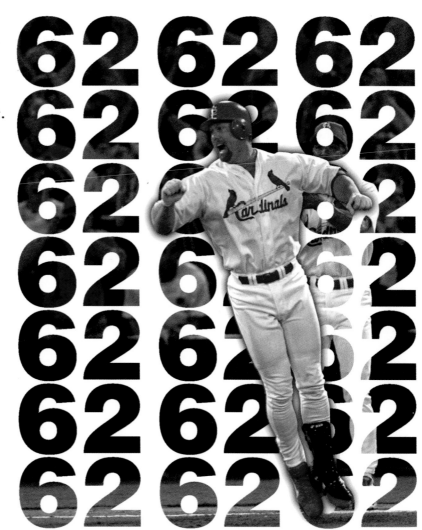

Mark McGwire celebrates after blasting his record-breaking 62nd home run of the season.

Big Hits in Little League

Breaking the home run record was a dream come true for the redheaded Californian, who had loved baseball since he was a child. "As a boy he'd lay on the floor watching baseball games on television," Mark's mother, Ginger, said. "He wouldn't take the trash out as long as there was a game on. He always had that dream of playing in the major leagues."

But his father, John, wouldn't let Mark play Little League ball at first. "I'd heard too much about arguing, meddling parents, and bad coaches," he said. "When I told him he couldn't play, he cried and cried and cried."

The next year, when Mark was eight, his father found a coach he liked and let Mark play. Mark was a power hitter from the beginning. In his first Little League at-bat, Mark hit a home run over a chicken-wire fence.

Mark was the pitcher on his team, but things didn't always go his way on the mound. During one game he walked so many batters he started to cry. His father, a coach, suggested he play shortstop for a while. "I can still remember looking in at the plate from shortstop, and everything was real fuzzy," Mark said. "I got glasses after that."

Mark's strong arm made him a star pitcher at Damien High School in Claremont, California. He didn't brag about his ability. He left his trophies in the back of his closet.

"I come from a family where you're never put on a pedestal, everybody's the same," Mark said. His four brothers also excelled in sports: Dan played quarterback for the Seattle Seahawks and Miami Dolphins, Bob was a star on the Citrus Community College golf team, Jay competed as a bodybuilder and Mike was a high school soccer player and golfer.

The boys gained inspiration from their father, who had polio as a child, causing one leg to be shorter than the other. Yet he bikes, golfs, and even boxed in college. Mark was a good enough pitcher to be chosen by the Montreal Expos in the eighth round of the June 1981 free-agent draft. But he decided to take advantage of a baseball scholarship offered to him by the University of Southern California.

Mark wasn't a bad pitcher, but what his team really needed was a power-hitting first baseman. So, like Babe Ruth before him, Mark went from the mound to being an everyday player. It was a good move. In 1984, he set a Pac-10 Conference record for most home runs in a season, with 32. He was named *The Sporting News'* 1984 College Player of the Year.

Mark impressed the Oakland Athletics so much that they chose him as the No. 10 pick in the first round in the 1984 draft. That summer Mark also starred on the U.S. Olympic baseball team.

A's Unleash Big Mac Attack

Mark's success on the baseball field came to an abrupt halt during his first minor league season at Class A Modesto in California. He got off to an awful start, playing in 16 games and batting .200. "I can remember lying in bed in the middle of the night," his ex-wife, Kathy Williamson, remembers, "and Mark saying, 'I can't hit the baseball anymore. I'm done. I've lost it. I've got to quit.'"

Mark doubted his ability, but he persevered. He spent the next season, 1985, as Modesto's starting third baseman and batted .274 with 24 homers. He won the California League's Rookie of the Year Award. The next season the Oakland A's called him up on August 20. He hit his first major league home run on August 25, off Walt Terrell of Detroit. However, he ended the season with a dismal .189 batting average and made six errors at third base.

McGwire breaks his bat but still manages a single.

As he had done in minor league ball, Mark put his hitting problems behind him during his first full season. Mark burst on the scene with a rookie-record 49 home runs and was the 1987 American League Rookie of the Year. He hit 33 home runs by the All-Star break, and the possibility of him breaking Maris' record was mentioned for the first time.

Mark had a chance to hit 50 home runs that year, but he decided not to play in the last game of the season. He flew home to be with his wife, Kathy, who was about to give birth to their son, Matthew. "I was thinking, 'I'll never have another first child, but I will have another chance to hit 50 home runs,'" Mark said.

Mark unleashes his power as he blasts one out of the park.

The Bash Brothers

Between 1988 and 1990, Mark and Jose Canseco helped Oakland enjoy three extremely successful seasons. They became known as "The Bash Brothers" because of the way they celebrated home runs by bashing their powerful forearms together.

Under the brilliant managing of Tony La Russa, the A's won three straight American League pennants. One of Mark's most memorable moments came in Game 3 of the 1988 World Series. In the ninth inning he hit a home run off Jay Howell, giving the A's a 2-1 victory against the Los Angeles Dodgers, Oakland's only win in the Series that year.

The next season the A's beat Bay area rival San Francisco in the World Series. But the title was marred by an earthquake in San Francisco.

"We had to respect what happened to northern California," Mark said. "We didn't get to celebrate." The next year, the Cincinnati Reds shocked the heavily favored A's by sweeping them in the World Series. Mark had only five hits in postseason play.

Opposite page: Mark McGwire bashes forearms with his teammates after hitting the game-winning home run during the third game of the 1988 World Series.

Some Pain, Some Gain

The 1991 season was the low point in Mark's major league career. He hit .201 with 22 home runs, breaking his streak of four years with at least 30 home runs. During the 1990 and 1991 seasons, he went 102 at-bats without a home run, the longest long-ball drought of his career.

La Russa took him out of the lineup at the end of the season so his average wouldn't fall below .200. Then Mark worked on his hitting and returned to weightlifting. Weightlifting has helped him hone his 6-foot-5, 250-pound body into a mass of muscle. His biceps are 20 inches around and his forearms measure 17 1/2 inches!

"Weightlifting relieved a lot of the pain I was going through following the '91 season," Mark said. "When I started to see the changes in my body, it made me feel a lot more positive, more confident in myself."

He also talked to a therapist and refused to feel sorry for himself. "I just decided that there wasn't any room for pouting or complaining or anything but my best," he said.

Mark hit 42 home runs in 1992. He got off to a great start in 1993, but a heel injury forced him to sit out all but 27 games that season. He still hit nine home runs, the second-best figure in major league history for a player with 100 or fewer at-bats. Another heel injury and a stiff back shortened his 1994 season to 47 games.

But Mark learned something while he was injured. "When I was injured in '93, it was the first time in my career I had to sit back and watch the game," he said. "Instead of sitting back and feeling sorry for myself, I started watching players, watching pitchers, watching how the game is played. It made me understand what the game is all about.

"You can only play this game on physical ability for so long. I'm just sorry it took my failure of '91 and the injuries of '93 and '94 for me to learn to use my mind."

McGwire speaks to reporters at a press conference. Notice his enormous biceps and forearms.

Healing, Hitting Homers

The baseball strike shortened the 1995 season to 144 games, but a healthy Mark didn't let that stop him. He hit 39 home runs, the most ever by a player with fewer than 392 at-bats. His average distance of 418 feet per homer was the best in the major leagues.

Mark hurt his heel again in 1996 and considered retiring. But, inspired by his father, he decided to continue playing. "I looked at all the injuries I've had throughout my career," he said. "My injuries are meaningless compared to what my father went through."

Mark made the right decision. That year he broke the Oakland home run record with a major league-leading 52 homers. He launched one into the fifth deck of the Toronto SkyDome. "That man is the strongest I've ever seen," Oakland manager Art Howe said, calling Mark's home runs "bombs."

As in 1995, Mark hit a home run every 8.13 at-bats, a major league record. His .312 batting average was his best ever. But Mark bristled when reporters asked him about breaking Maris' record.

"I'm not close to anything," he said in August, when he had already hit 43 home runs. "I don't know what the big deal is."

Meet Me in St. Louis

Mark got off to a great start in 1997. He hit 11 home runs in April, the most ever in the month for an Oakland player. In four months with the A's he hit 34 home runs. But he shook his head when he was compared with Babe Ruth. "It blows me away," Mark said. "I say to myself, 'You've got to be kidding me.'"

In the middle of the season he went into a home run slump that lasted 71 at-bats. On July 31, Mark was traded to the St. Louis Cardinals and reunited with his old manager, La Russa. Mark and the Cardinals were a match made in baseball heaven. The city loved baseball and it embraced the gentle giant.

Mark also showed the city his warm side. When he signed a contract extension, he donated more than $1 million to help abused and neglected children. It didn't take long for Mark's home run bat to reheat. On August 8, against Philadelphia, he hit a 441-foot home run during his first game as a Cardinal in Busch Stadium. He set a club record with 15 homers in September.

The Cardinals began letting fans into the stadium earlier than normal so they could watch Mark launch torpedoes into the seats during batting practice. Everyone in the stadium, including teammates and opposing players, would watch him take batting practice. The Cardinals pitchers even changed their pre-game meeting time.

"There are power hitters, and then there is Mark McGwire," Cardinals catcher Tom Pagnozzi said. "He's way beyond anybody else in this game."

Mark ended the season with a home run burst, with three in the last weekend to bring his season total to 58. That was the most in the majors since Maris hit 61 in 1961. At that time, only Mark and Babe Ruth had hit more than 50 home runs in consecutive seasons. Mark became the first player to hit 20 home runs for two teams in the same season.

The season left Mark exhausted. He called it "the most grinding, mind-grueling season I've ever endured. My mind felt more exhausted than my body."

Tony La Russa (left) gives Mark a hug after finishing the season with the Cardinals after coming over from Oakland.

Chasing History

Talk of Mark breaking the home run record only intensified early in 1998. "Mark is one of those players who is so special, you cannot put limits on what he can do," La Russa said during spring training. "He might hit 40, 50, or 60 this year. He might hit 70."

Mark admitted it was possible for him to break the record. "I've always appreciated how difficult it is and now I know how possible it is," he said. "I hit 58 (last season) and had a terrible July. But it would have to be almost a perfect season for it to happen."

Mark didn't disappoint his many fans. He hit home runs in his first four games and three on April 14 and May 19. On May 16, Mark hit a 545-foot shot that smacked against a sign above the outfield fence at Busch Stadium. The Cardinals covered the mark with a giant Band-Aid. Before September even began, he had hit five home runs of more than 500 feet.

"When he hits one, you hear the (fans) buzz for 10 or 15 or 20 minutes," La Russa said. "In St. Louis, it goes on for two or three innings."

The home run chase revived interest in baseball and gave the nation a new hero to root for. Fans from opposing teams cheered Mark's home runs, begging him for curtain calls. After Chicago

White Sox rookie Jim Parque gave up home run No. 30 to Mark, he walked Mark the next time he came to bat. The hometown crowd booed its own pitcher. "You can't win," Parque said.

Batting practice became a must-see event everywhere Mark played. "There's probably more pressure on me in batting practice now than there is in the game," Mark said jokingly. "Where does the attraction between me and fans come from? I don't know. But you know what? This game needs more excitement. If my batting practice brings more people out to the game, it's good."

Mark takes a moment to acknowledge his fans.

But the ever-increasing attention from the media and fans sometimes bothered Mark. "It's all very, very overwhelming," he said. "The whole thing is just 1,000 times more than it's ever been, which is a little uncomfortable. I've been recognized my whole career, but now I just can't go anywhere."

Mark wasn't the only one chasing Maris' record that season. Sosa, Ken Griffey Jr., and Greg Vaughn were also in the hunt. By early September, Sosa and Mark both had 55 home runs. But it was a friendly rivalry. "I always say to myself that the man to do it is Mark McGwire," Sosa said. "I've got my money on him."

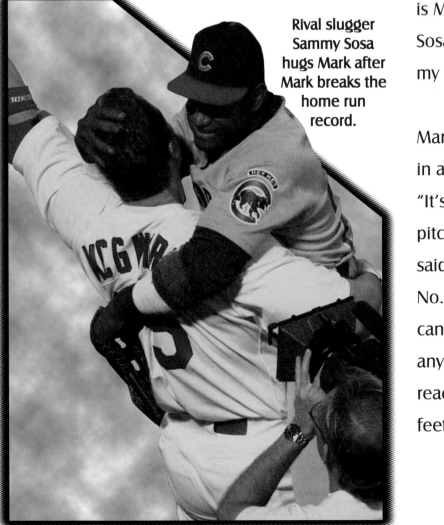

Rival slugger Sammy Sosa hugs Mark after Mark breaks the home run record.

Sosa wasn't Mark's only opponent in awe of his power. "It's amazing," Florida pitcher Rob Stanifer said after giving up No. 59 to Mark. "You can't throw the guy any pitch he can reach or he hits it 500 feet."

Spirit of St. Louis

On September 7, in an afternoon game against the Cubs in St. Louis, Mark launched home run No. 61 to tie Maris' record. The 430-foot blast landed just inside the left field foul pole. "As soon as it left my bat, I just threw my hands up," Mark said. "I knew it at that time. What a feeling that was."

Mark pointed to the sky and tapped his heart in honor of Maris. He raised his fist in the air as he jogged triumphantly around the bases, receiving hugs from his opponents. More than 50,000 fans in Busch Stadium stood and roared. After Mark hopped onto home plate, he lifted his son into the air and hugged him.

Mark's parents, Ginger and John, congratulate their son after he tied Roger Maris' home run record of 61.

Mark knew the record could soon be his. "I'm one swing away," he said. The next night, his line drive to left field again drove the St. Louis crowd into a frenzy. The home run record was his!

But Mark wasn't done yet. He hit 70 home runs that season, including five in the last three days to win the spirited duel with Sosa for the new home run record. Mark's total astounded even the big slugger himself.

"To say the least, I amazed myself," Mark said. "I think (the record) will stand for a while."

"My next big career goal is to hit 500 home runs," he said. "If I stay healthy like I have the past few years and I put up the numbers that I'm capable of, who knows how many more home runs I'll hit?"

Mark watches as homer number 62 clears the wall.

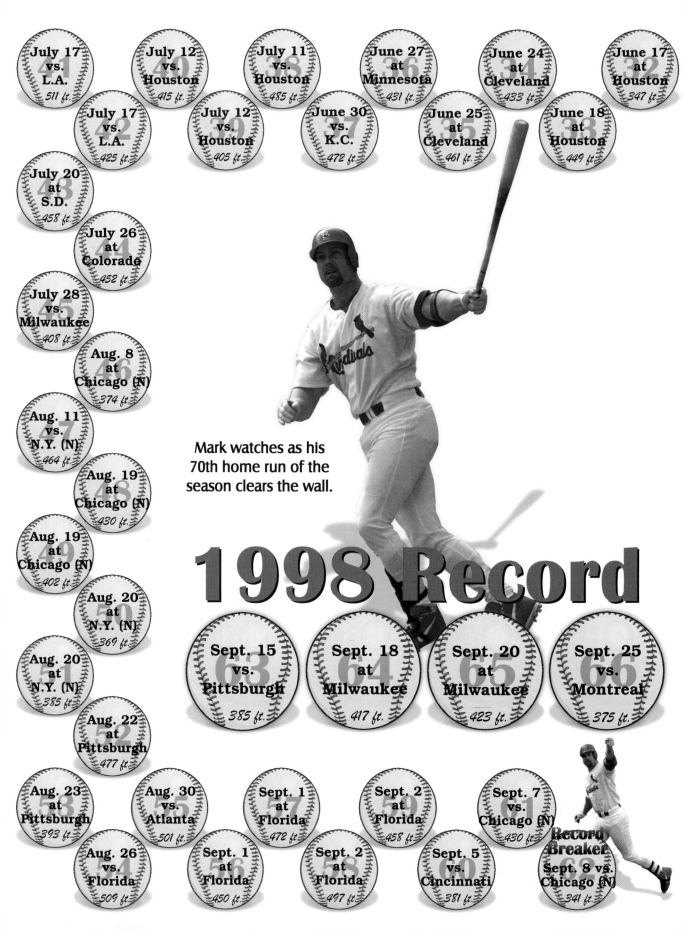

July 17 vs. L.A. **41** 511 ft.

July 12 vs. Houston **40** 415 ft.

July 11 vs. Houston **38** 485 ft.

June 27 at Minnesota **36** 431 ft.

June 24 at Cleveland **34** 433 ft.

June 17 at Houston **32** 347 ft.

July 17 vs. L.A. **42** 425 ft.

July 12 vs. Houston **39** 405 ft.

June 30 vs. K.C. **37** 472 ft.

June 25 at Cleveland **35** 461 ft.

June 18 at Houston **33** 449 ft.

July 20 at S.D. **43** 458 ft.

July 26 at Colorado **44** 452 ft.

July 28 vs. Milwaukee **45** 408 ft.

Aug. 8 at Chicago (N) **46** 374 ft.

Aug. 11 vs. N.Y. (N) **47** 464 ft.

Aug. 19 at Chicago (N) **48** 430 ft.

Aug. 19 at Chicago (N) **49** 402 ft.

Aug. 20 at N.Y. (N) **50** 369 ft.

Aug. 20 at N.Y. (N) **51** 385 ft.

Aug. 22 at Pittsburgh **52** 477 ft.

Aug. 23 at Pittsburgh **53** 393 ft.

Aug. 30 vs. Atlanta **55** 501 ft.

Sept. 1 at Florida **57** 472 ft.

Sept. 2 at Florida **59** 458 ft.

Sept. 7 vs. Chicago (N) **61** 430 ft.

Aug. 26 vs. Florida **54** 509 ft.

Sept. 1 at Florida **56** 450 ft.

Sept. 2 at Florida **58** 497 ft.

Sept. 5 vs. Cincinnati **60** 381 ft.

Mark watches as his 70th home run of the season clears the wall.

1998 Record

Sept. 15 vs. Pittsburgh **63** 385 ft.

Sept. 18 at Milwaukee **64** 417 ft.

Sept. 20 at Milwaukee **65** 423 ft.

Sept. 25 vs. Montreal **66** 375 ft.

Record Breaker Sept. 8 vs. Chicago (N) **62** 341 ft.

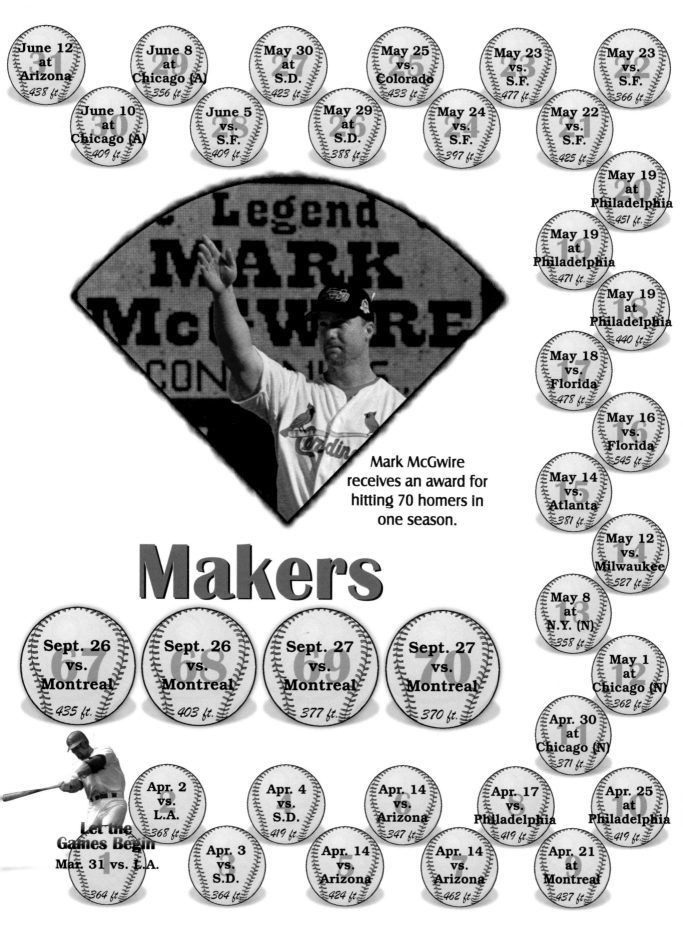

June 12
at
Arizona
31
438 ft.

June 8
at
Chicago (A)
29
356 ft.

May 30
at
S.D.
27
423 ft.

May 25
vs.
Colorado
25
433 ft.

May 23
vs.
S.F.
23
477 ft.

May 23
vs.
S.F.
22
366 ft.

June 10
at
Chicago (A)
30
409 ft.

June 5
vs.
S.F.
28
409 ft.

May 29
at
S.D.
26
388 ft.

May 24
vs.
S.F.
24
397 ft.

May 22
vs.
S.F.
21
425 ft.

May 19
at
Philadelphia
20
451 ft.

May 19
at
Philadelphia
19
471 ft.

May 19
at
Philadelphia
18
440 ft.

May 18
vs.
Florida
17
478 ft.

May 16
vs.
Florida
16
545 ft.

May 14
vs.
Atlanta
15
381 ft.

May 12
vs.
Milwaukee
14
527 ft.

May 8
at
N.Y. (N)
13
358 ft.

May 1
at
Chicago (N)
12
362 ft.

Apr. 30
at
Chicago (N)
11
371 ft.

Legend MARK McGWIRE

Mark McGwire receives an award for hitting 70 homers in one season.

Makers

Sept. 26
vs.
Montreal
67
435 ft.

Sept. 26
vs.
Montreal
68
403 ft.

Sept. 27
vs.
Montreal
69
377 ft.

Sept. 27
vs.
Montreal
70
370 ft.

Let the
Games Begin
Mar. 31 vs. L.A.
1
364 ft.

Apr. 2
vs.
L.A.
2
368 ft.

Apr. 4
vs.
S.D.
4
419 ft.

Apr. 14
vs.
Arizona
6
347 ft.

Apr. 17
vs.
Philadelphia
8
419 ft.

Apr. 25
at
Philadelphia
10
419 ft.

Apr. 3
vs.
S.D.
3
364 ft.

Apr. 14
vs.
Arizona
5
424 ft.

Apr. 14
vs.
Arizona
7
462 ft.

Apr. 21
at
Montreal
9
437 ft.

Mark McGwire Profile

Born: October 1, 1963, in

　　　Pomona, California

Resides: Long Beach, California

Height: 6-5

Weight: 250 lbs

Bats: Right

Throws: Right

Personal: Is single and has one son, Matthew. His brother, Dan, was a quarterback for the Miami Dolphins and Seattle Seahawks.

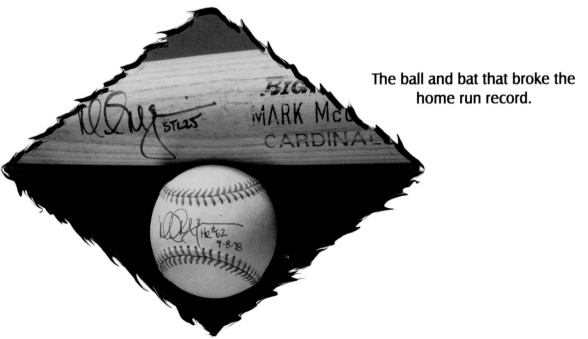

The ball and bat that broke the home run record.

Honors

The Sporting News College Player of the Year, 1984

The Sporting News All-America Team, 1984

California League Rookie of the Year, 1985

American League Rookie of the Year, 1987

Rawlings Gold Glove, 1990

The Sporting News All-Star Team, 1992

UPI All-Star Team, 1992

UPI Comeback Player of the Year, 1992

Named to Silver Slugger Team, 1996

Associated Press All-Star Team, 1996

Named to the American League All-Star Team (nine times)

American League Player of
   the Month, June 1996

National League Player of
   the Week (four times)

National League Player of
   the Month (four times)

Named to the National
   League All-Star Team, 1998

Chronology

October 1, 1963 - Born in Pomona, California.

June 1981 - Graduates from Damien High School in Claremont, California. Selected by the Montreal Expos in the eighth round of the free-agent draft but doesn't sign.

September 1981 - Begins first of three years at the University of Southern California, attending on a baseball scholarship.

June 1984 - Selected by the Oakland A's in the first round, the No. 10 pick overall, of the free-agent draft.

Summer 1984 - Plays for the U.S. Olympic baseball team.

1985 - Plays third base and hits 24 home runs at Class A Modesto, earning California League Rookie of the Year Award.

1986 - Plays for Huntsville (Alabama) and Tacoma (Washington) in the minor leagues before being called up to Oakland on August 20. Gets first major league hit on August 24, first major league home run on August 25.

1987 - Hits 49 home runs to set major league rookie record, leads American League and ties Cubs' Andre Dawson for major league high. Named AL Rookie of the Year.

1988 - Hits home run in ninth inning of Game 3 of World Series to give A's 2-1 win over Los Angeles.

1992 - Leads major leagues with one home run for every 11.1 at-bats, hitting 42 for the season.

1995 - Hits 39 home runs, most home runs ever by a player with fewer than 392 at-bats (Hank Aaron hit 40 home runs in 392 at-bats in 1973).

1996 - Hits a Oakland-record 52 home runs, which leads the major leagues. Sets major league record with one home run for every 8.13 at-bats.

July 31, 1997 - Traded to the St. Louis Cardinals for pitchers T.J. Mathews, Eric Ludwick, and Blake Stein.

1997 - Hits 58 home runs, tying major league record for most home runs in a season by a right-handed batter. Becomes the second major-leaguer (with Babe Ruth) to hit 50 or more home runs in consecutive seasons, and the first to hit 20 home runs with two teams in a season.

1998 - Ties Roger Maris' single-season home run record on September 7, and breaks it by hitting home run No. 62 on September 8. Finishes with major-league record 70 home runs and career high 147 RBI.

907074

Mark's Major League Stats

Year	Team	Batting Average	Home Runs
1986	Oakland	.189	3
1987	Oakland	.289	49
1988	Oakland	.260	32
1989	Oakland	.231	33
1990	Oakland	.235	39
1991	Oakland	.201	22
1992	Oakland	.268	42
1993	Oakland	.333	9
1994	Oakland	.252	9
1995	Oakland	.274	39
1996	Oakland	.312	52
1997	Oakland/St. Louis	.268	58
1998	St. Louis	.299	70

Glossary

BATTING AVERAGE - The number of hits a batter gets divided by the number of times at bat.

BICEPS - A large muscle in the front of the upper arm.

CURTAIN CALL - To emerge from the dugout and wave to the crowd in response to the fans' continued applause.

DUGOUT - A covered place for managers, coaches, and players to sit when they are not at bat or in the field.

ERROR - A mistake by a fielder that allows a batter to reach base or lets a runner take an extra base.

FOREARM - The part of the arm between the wrist and elbow.

HOME RUN - A ball hit far enough that the batter touches all the bases and scores a run.

MAJOR LEAGUES - The top level in a professional sport. In baseball, the American League and National League make up the major leagues.

MINOR LEAGUE - A league below the major leagues, made up of organized teams that are part of major league teams' organizations.

POLIO - A disease that can paralyze muscles.

ROOKIE - A person playing his first full year of baseball in the minor or major leagues.

STRIKE - To swing at a ball and miss, or to not swing at a ball in the strike zone. A ball hit foul but not caught in the air is also a strike when the batter has less than two strikes.

WORLD SERIES - A series of games between the top team in the American League and National League to determine the champion.

Index